Sabbath Rest

Look for these topics in the Everyday Matters Bible Studies for Women

Acceptance	Mentoring
Bible Study & Meditation	Outreach
Celebration	Prayer
Community	Reconciliation
Confession	Sabbath Rest
Contemplation	Service
Faith	Silence
Fasting	Simplicity
Forgiveness	Solitude
Gratitude	Stewardship
Hospitality	Submission
Justice	Worship

Sabbath Rest

Spiritual Practices
FOR EVERYDAY LIFE

**Everyday Matters Bible Studies for Women—
Sabbath Rest**

© 2014 Hendrickson Publishers Marketing, LLC
P. O. Box 3473
Peabody, Massachusetts 01961-3473

ISBN 978-1-61970-575-3

Printed in the United States of America

First Printing — December 2014

Contents

Holy Habits

Spiritual Practices for Everyday Life

Everyday life today is busier and more distracting than it has ever been before. While cell phones and texting make it easier to keep track of children and each other, they also make it harder to get away from the demands that overwhelm us. Time, it seems, is a shrinking commodity. But God, the Creator of time, has given us the keys to leading a life that may be challenging but not overwhelming. In fact, he offers us tools to do what seems impossible and come away refreshed and renewed. These tools are called spiritual practices, or spiritual disciplines.

Spiritual practices are holy habits. They are rooted in God's word, and they go back to creation itself. God has hardwired us to thrive when we obey him, even when it seems like his instructions defy our "common sense." When we engage in the holy habits that God has ordained, time takes on a new dimension. What seems impossible is actually easy; it's easy because we are tapping into God's resources.

The holy habits that we call spiritual practices are all geared to position us in a place where we can allow the Holy Spirit to work in us and through us, to grant us power and strength to do the things we can't do on our own. They take us to a place where we can become intimate with God.

While holy habits and everyday life may sound like opposites, they really aren't.

As you learn to incorporate spiritual practices into your life, you'll find that everyday life is easier. At the same time, you will draw closer to God and come to a place where you can luxuriate in his rich blessings. Here is a simple example. Elizabeth Collings hated running household errands. Picking up dry cleaning, doing the grocery shopping, and chauffeuring her kids felt like a never-ending litany of menial chores. One day she had a simple realization that changed her life. That day she began to use her "chore time" as a time of prayer and fellowship with God.

Whenever Elizabeth walked the aisle of the supermarket, she prayed for each person who would eat the item of food she selected. On her way to pick up her children, she would lay their lives out before God, asking him to be there for them even when she couldn't. Each errand became an opportunity for fellowship with God. The chore that had been so tedious became a precious part of her routine that she cherished.

The purpose of these study guides is to help you use spiritual practices to make your own life richer, fuller, and deeper. The series includes twenty-four spiritual practices that are the building blocks of Christian spiritual formation. Each practice is a holy habit that has been modeled for us in the Bible. The practices are acceptance, Bible study and meditation, celebration, community, confession, contemplation, faith, fasting, forgiveness, gratitude, hospitality, justice, mentoring, outreach, prayer, reconciliation, Sabbath rest, service, silence, simplicity, solitude, stewardship, submission, and worship.

As you move through the practices that you select, remember Christ's promise in Matthew 11:28–30:

> *Come to me, all of you who are weary and carry heavy burdens. Take my yoke upon you. Let me teach you, because I am humble and gentle at heart, and you will find rest for your souls. For my yoke is easy to bear, and the burden I give you is light.*

Introduction

to the Practice of Sabbath Rest

"The key to the Sabbath isn't merely rest.
Rather it's that in our rest we turn our attention
to God, whose rest our Sabbath mirrors."

—Lauren F. Winner

It's ironic, and possibly laughable, that we humans can't
seem to rest without being told to do so. From the time
our language skills kick in, we resist rest. We refuse to take
naps, take a break, or take a vacation. And so even in this
simple act of *not* doing, we must be told what to not do.

Depending on the day, most of us would say all we want is to
rest, and we wish we could. When we talk about rest, though,
we generally don't mean a Sabbath rest. We don't mean a restorative wholeness, a putting right of our lives and relationships. I suspect what we generally are going for is relief. The
project at hand is hard, even if we're being paid to do it. A
relationship gets rocky, and though we've no plan to abandon
it, a little break from the tension would be awfully nice.

It's easy to imagine God knowing we'd do this badly,
and in his wisdom, he placed rest right there in the Ten

Commandments so we wouldn't miss it. If that wasn't enough, a quick search of your Bible concordance will show 147 Bible verses addressing the Sabbath. Clearly the Sabbath is a big deal to God. Yet when we as a people need to be told to rest, it's a sure sign we will figure out a way to make rest less like rest, a Sabbath less like worship, and more like work. As Jonalyn Fincher says in "Mary Magdalene: Meeting the Risen Lord" (*Everyday Matters Bible for Women*), "Most of us believe rest is for the weary and faint, the overwhelmed, the sick or depressed. We rest because we're forced into it, not because we're invited." So our tendency, from the beginning, has been to find a way to make it more about us and less about God.

By the first century, the Jews had been busy codifying for centuries what rest was and was not. Estimates vary, but it's generally accepted that at least thirty-nine groupings of activities were prohibited on the Sabbath. It became a day of "cannots" and "shoulds" rather than a day of celebrating the freedom and generosity of a life with God. Part of this might be because on the surface, the Jews (and us Christians) "are not convinced rest is as spiritual as God made it out to be," Jonalyn Fincher writes. Our goal, as we study the concept of Sabbath rest, will be to redeem it from this legacy and to restore our mind-set of God's amazing gift. It might be a commandment, but it's embedded with the love of a Father, who eagerly desires to give good gifts to his children. And we start with the good news that the Sabbath does bring relief—but it also brings more. As a spiritual discipline it can create a rhythmic pattern of ceasing our own efforts so we may turn our attention to God.

So where can we look for guidance on Sabbath-keeping? Certainly we look to the Scriptures. And yet as we look at those 147 verses about the Sabbath, we must resist the temptation to create a checklist of "don'ts" for our Sabbath rest. Instead, let us create a framework of "dos," and a foundation solidly planted in God's motivations for the Sabbath.

Though many people see Amish lives as restrictive and resistant to change, the Amish see their choices as the result of examining life closely, and their practices bear consideration for us as we begin to look at God's commands for Sabbath rest. As Suzanne Woods Fisher writes in *Amish Peace: Simple Living for a Complicated World* (Revell Books, 2009):

> *When something new reaches into the Amish community, the church leaders might give it a period of probation, weighing out its long-term effects, and each church district comes to its own conclusions. And, always, the church leaders consider where a change could lead the younger generation. They try to see beyond the immediate benefits of change to the affects it could have down the road. How could this new technology or gadget tempt someone away from the church? Or to disobey God?*

What if we examined the choices we make, each one on its ability to draw us closer to God and each other? What would we leave behind? What would we rearrange? What would we embrace?

As Ginger Kolbaba writes in "The Ignored Commandment" (*Everyday Matters Bible for Women*), may our studies bring us to "turn to God in obedience, trusting him with our schedules and responsibilities, enjoying his blessings of delight, rest, and play."

CHAPTER 1

Remembering the "Apples"

Our Image-Bearing Identity

So the creation of the heavens and the earth and
everything in them was completed. On the seventh
day God had finished his work of creation, so he
rested from all his work. And God blessed the
seventh day and declared it holy, because it was the
day when he rested from all his work of creation.

GENESIS 2:1-3

For this study, read Psalm 92.

As a child, a good friend of mine left home each day to
these words: "Remember the apples." Her mother would call
them out as the door opened into her day, making sure the
last words her children heard as they exited the house or
car, were a reminder of their true identity.

The family didn't grow apples, at least not literally. The
apples were a catchphrase for a quote we've heard in its full
measure: "The apple doesn't fall far from the tree." For my

friend's mother, it was a reminder that you are a reflection of your family. You bear the imprint of a family tree. You've been given every good gift from it, and you are meant to offer good things to the world. Make sure your life bears, as it should, the right image of this tree.

From the beginning, God has told us the same thing. Twice in the first chapter of Genesis, it is clear whose image we bear. In Genesis 1:26 we read, "Then God said, 'Let us make human beings in our image, to be like us.'" The idea is repeated again in Genesis 1:27:

> So God created human beings in his own image.
>   In the image of God he created them;
>   male and female he created them.

We are told from the beginning what our lives should reflect. It's a big concept, one that will take us a lifetime to accomplish—just as God intended.

Part of our image-bearing mandate is rest. In Exodus 20:8–11, as God gives the Ten Commandments to Moses, he links our rest to his rest:

> "Remember to observe the Sabbath day by keeping it holy. You have six days each week for your ordinary work, but the seventh day is a Sabbath day of rest dedicated to the LORD your God. On that day no one in your household may do any work. This includes you, your sons and daughters, your male and female servants, your livestock, and any foreigners living among you. For in six days the LORD made the heavens, the earth, the sea, and everything in them; but on the seventh day he rested. That is why the LORD blessed the Sabbath day and set it apart as holy."

This is rest, not because we feel like it or have a break in our schedule. This is the rest of obedience and humility—and one that is ours only because of our relationship with God. And it's a day dedicated to the Lord; a day of no work, and a day where we don't create work for others. Instead, Sabbath rest gives us a chance to reflect on God's provision, on God's attributes, and on God's love. It gives us a chance to know more about the God whose image we bear. And what can we learn from how God participated in the Sabbath? In Genesis 1:31, God has finished his work. What does he do? "Then God looked over all he had made, and he saw that it was very good!"

Part and parcel of the Sabbath is celebration of the work we have done. As did God, we look back at our six days; we celebrate our good work and the chance to do good work. We thank God for the work to come, and we take a needed rest. By doing so, we can offer an image of God to a watching world. Create, then rest. Produce, then rest. Care for others, then rest. Together, the working and the resting create worship.

"There are some things that can be accomplished, even by God, only in a state of rest." —Eugene Peterson

> *As you study this chapter, consider your own ideas of what the Sabbath is and is for. How much of it seems to be about restricting your actions? How much of it is about realizing who you are?*

1. Exodus 20:10 conveys the commandment not only of our own rest but also rest for all, humans and animals, living with us. In Exodus 23:12, God again points out the need for rest for everyone and likens our rest to a restorative act of justice. How does this become a way to bear the image of God to others?

2. What obstacles are present in your life now to the practice of a Sabbath day of rest?

3. In Jeremiah 6:16, God points the people of Israel to look back: "Ask for the old, godly way, and walk in it. Travel its path, and you will find rest for your souls." Think back on your own earlier practices or perhaps the practices of family members in the past. What ways did they have of observing the Sabbath?

4. In "A Steady Rhythm" (*Everyday Matters Bible for Women*), Ruth Haley Barton suggests that God's command to rest on the Sabbath was "a way of giving the seventh day back to God like a tithe of one's time." How would viewing a Sabbath rest as a giving back to God the firstfruits of your week help you?

5. Read Ezekiel 20:12–16. What does God say the Sabbath is a sign of? What does it yield if we obey the command to observe the Sabbath? What happens when we reject the command?

6. When you think of the attributes of God, is "Sabbath-keeper" one that comes to mind? Looking at Genesis 1, what are all the things you can know about God from the first chapter of the Bible?

Points to Ponder

It's easy to believe that our struggle to observe the Sabbath is harder now, with more temptations at our fingertips and fewer societal constraints. And while the particulars of our lives differ from biblical times, the urge to skip rest and keep working seems to be a universal, ongoing issue. As Ginger Kolbaba notes in "The Ignored Commandment" (*Everyday Matters Bible for Women*), both Nehemiah and Ezekiel confronted the Israelites about breaking the Sabbath command (Nehemiah 13:15–22; Ezekiel 20:1–6; 22:8). And in a particularly condemning passage of Amos 8, God promises destruction in part because of their eagerness to end a Sabbath and get back to the business of buying and selling (and cheating each other!). We are not immune to the temptations to ignore the Sabbath, but neither are we the first.

- Pray about what in your life may be breaking the Sabbath command.

- Seek ways then to surrender those things so you may truly enter God's rest.

"True rest is found in submitting to God's will, in obeying his direction. It is when we place our trust in God and align ourselves to the 'old, godly way' that we find both rest and renewed strength."
—*Kelli B. Trujillo, "A Benefit of Obedience,"* Everyday Matters Bible for Women

Prayer

Lord, the Sabbath is yours, just as all my days are yours. Nothing happens without your power and presence in my life. I want my days to sing, with the writers of the psalms, about your goodness and faithfulness. Thank you for the rest you offer me.

Add your prayer in your own words.

Amen.

Put It into Practice

Take a look at your calendar for the last month. Acknowledging that you are an image-bearer, what image does your calendar reflect? What do the activities and the empty spaces say about God and his presence in your life? What needs to change to more accurately reflect your relationship with God?

Take-away Treasure

Psalm 92 begins with a note to the reader, "A song to be sung on the Sabbath Day." It is a song of praise and thanks—and is filled only with the deeds of God. Perhaps the reorientation of our identity starts with singing, along with the psalmist, "It is good to proclaim your unfailing love in the morning, your faithfulness in the evening" (v. 2). If God's attributes include unfailing love and faithfulness, how can your week—all seven days—more accurately reflect that to a watching world?

CHAPTER 2

Free Time and Freedom

Victory over the Tyranny of the Urgent

> "Remember that you were once slaves in Egypt, but the Lᴏʀᴅ your God brought you out with his strong hand and powerful arm. That is why the Lᴏʀᴅ your God has commanded you to rest on the Sabbath day."
>
> DEUTERONOMY 5:15

For this study, read Psalm 127.

When my children were little, I made a hard, unpopular decision. There would be no activities on Sunday other than church. No birthday parties, no athletics, no child asking, "Can you drive me to Nathan's for a play date?" And that was so hard. As a working mom, my children basically lived on my schedule all week—they became commuters at an early age, getting up and ready to go so I could catch a train, staying at the babysitters after school until I could arrive back. They were great about it, every single day. So with only two days to shift the schedule each week, how could

I take one half of it and say no? Well, it was desperation. It was the realization that I felt every single stitch of time had been spent, every single week, and that felt a great deal like slavery. I needed a day where I never had to look at a clock.

There is absolutely nothing better than waking up on a day off from work, feeling unfettered and free to do as we choose. Even as we stretch out and turn over for just a few more minutes of sleep, our day seems to stretch out as well, full of possibilities.

And there is nothing worse, having embraced our freedom, than looking at the calendar and finding we're committed to any number of things. The chains wrap our wrists and our mind once more, and all of a sudden our day off looks and feels entirely different.

To be enslaved to something means our resources—time and money, even our thoughts—are not ours to do with as we choose. It means we must consult with someone else before using them. It's easy to see why Jonathan Swift could easily point to our complicated relationship with time in *Gulliver's Travels*. Speaking of Gulliver, the Lilliputians report that "he put this engine [pocket watch] into our ears, which made an incessant noise, like that of a water-mill: and we conjecture it is either some unknown animal or the god that he worships; but we are more inclined to the latter opinion, because he assured us . . . that he seldom did any-thing without consulting it."

I wince when I read those words. As I look around me, I can see four timepieces, all of which I have consulted in the last thirty minutes. Within my reach are at least three more. The need to check the time, allot my time, and not waste my time is so prevalent that I don't even think about it. Yet I should. Anything I'm consulting that often, thinking about that much, certainly has the potential to become my god.

The second rendering of the Ten Commandments in Deuteronomy 5 has one significant change from the earlier version in Exodus 20: the *reason* for the fourth commandment. In all other respects God issues the same commands, except when it comes to observing the Sabbath. Our identity as image-bearers remains, but added to it is our status as free people.

It's a status easy to take for granted here in America. Of course we are free! But for the Israelites, freedom was only just returning after a long bondage in Egypt. As Eugene Peterson notes in *Working the Angles*, "Our ancestors in Egypt went four hundred years without a vacation. Never a day off. The consequence: they were no longer considered persons but slaves."

The consequence of not taking a day of rest remains for us too. When we refuse the Sabbath, we acknowledge we're not in charge, really. Our time is. And our only worth is our functionality, not our existence. So the Sabbath is a reminder of what God has done for us and how *he* sees us. He redeemed us from the slavery of sin and death, most definitely. But he also freed our days from the tyranny of the clock and the calendar. He freed us from living by them in ways that restrict and isolate us from him and the community of faith.

When God redeemed the Israelite's lives, he redeemed their time. Free people look at time differently than slaves. It's a gift and a tool and its unrestricted use is a symbol of their freedom.

When we ignore God's Sabbath rest, it's as if we have sold our birthright. We become less like God and less like ourselves. What happens when we won't stop and rest? We become addicted to our own productivity. We refuse to cede control of our lives to the One who, whether we acknowledge it or not, is in control. Our need for true worship goes unfulfilled, and so we fill the need with whatever is close at hand: money, sex, or power.

The discipline of the Sabbath is an act of freedom, not an act of independence. It is the intentional act of a free person, one not owned by others, nor enslaved by the desire for security or status. It is the act of a person who has found, in God, a joyful resting place.

As you study this chapter, consider the things that drive you to continue your work. What do you fear will happen if you stop? What are you beholden to?

1. In Exodus 16:23, God provides the needs of the day even on a day of rest in the wilderness. Consider your day of rest. What do you need? Can you trust God enough to provide it?

2. In Leviticus 25, God outlines conditions of rest for the year of jubilee. How would a practice such as that—freeing others, forgiving all debts, resting the land—change how you view your work and relationships?

3. We may not have Egyptian taskmasters assigning a quota of bricks to produce, but most of us do have to work within the goals and expectations set by others. What perspective can you gain from Psalm 127:2?

4. In Leviticus 23:3, we read God's injunction to observe the Sabbath day "wherever you live." Do you find when your location or routine changes, the first thing to go is your Sabbath? We go on vacation, we need travel for work or family obligations, and suddenly the Sabbath vanishes. How can you safeguard against it?

5. In "Addicted to Productivity" (*Everyday Matters Bible for Women*), Susan Arico suggests: "Instead of wedging more and more into our time, with our lives becoming like the crowded closet, we can rest well knowing that God wants to rescue us from this overwhelming and claustrophobic way of being." When you think of how you manage your time, what kind of image comes to mind? Would it be like a closet, crammed with too much? Or would it be a well-ordered, spacious place?

6. Ruth Haley Barton reminds us in "A Steady Rhythm" (*Everyday Matters Bible for Women*) that "Jesus taught his disciples to rest even from the good work of ministry." In Mark 6:31, Jesus invites them, "Let's go off by ourselves to a quiet place and rest awhile." What about you? Do you put your ministry efforts in a different category than other kinds of work?

"Take from our souls the strain and stress,
And let our ordered lives confess
The beauty of Thy peace."
—John Greenleaf Whittier

Points to Ponder

God uses the phrase "You have six days to do all your work" several times in his word. God is not unaware of the work before you, but he understands how much we need the regular rhythm of rest in our lives. We aren't the only entities that God set parameters on. In Psalm 74:17, Asaph says to God, "You set the boundaries of the earth, and you made both summer and winter." God's world is an ordered world, with seasons and day and evening. We often want to extend past our boundaries, whether it's spending more than we earn, working late into the evening, or putting off rest for any number of reasons.

- When we stop at the boundaries placed by a loving Father, what is the result?

- Can we accept our humanity and be grateful that our lives do not all depend on us?

"When we keep a Sabbath holy, we are practicing, for a day, the freedom that God intends for all people." —Dorothy C. Bass

Prayer

God, I am grateful you have freed me—you have freed me from the need to be the answer to every problem, from the idea that I alone provide for my life. You have freed me from being a slave to a small life of idol worship and placed me in your presence so I may truly worship. Thank you for the Sabbath day.

Add your prayer in your own words.

Amen.

Put It into Practice

In Matthew 11:28–30, Jesus offers to all the freedom of a life of rest:

> *Come to me, all of you who are weary and carry heavy burdens, and I will give you rest. Take my yoke upon you. Let me teach you, because I am humble and gentle at heart, and you will find rest for your souls. For my yoke is easy to bear, and the burden I give you is light.*

Today, consider the expansive space of the Sabbath—twenty-four hours of rest for the weary, the rest of a free person—and accept it.

Take-away Treasure

In "A Woman of Virtue: Living within Healthy Limits" (*Everyday Matters Bible for Women*), Adele Ahlberg Calhoun suggests that "living in sanity and spiritual health isn't simply about industry; it's about honoring our limits and embracing healthy margins." Today, look at your calendar and consider the margins of your days. Does every commitment, every task come hard on the heels of the one before it? Are there any free blocks of time, any margin for rest? This week, this month, let's place the margins before we place the commitments. Block out time that is just going to be free time. Use your Sabbath as a "clock free" zone, where you don't have to even look at the time, and remember the freedom God has given you.

CHAPTER 3

Bending In Our Favor

Time Teaches Us about Eternity

> Yet God has made everything beautiful for its
> own time. He has planted eternity in the human
> heart, but even so, people cannot see the whole
> scope of God's work from beginning to end.
>
> ECCLESIASTES 3:11

For this study, read Revelation 21.

Several years ago, I completely forfeited a vacation to illness. I had worked longer hours in the month leading up to the vacation, promising myself a good long rest at the appointed time—meaning, of course, the time *I* had deemed available. And rest I did. Yes, indeed, I barely left my bed. My body reminded me of something God has said to me, his beloved, from the very beginning: rest cannot be saved up. It must be embraced regularly. That missed vacation became the catalyst for redeeming Sabbath rest in my own life. I started reading through all the Scriptures related to the Sabbath, realizing that the only teaching I really knew was the fourth commandment.

In both Exodus 31 and 35, God's punishment for those who do not observe the Sabbath is unequivocal:

> *"You must keep the Sabbath day, for it is a holy day for you.*
> *Anyone who desecrates it must be put to death; anyone who*
> *works on that day will be cut off from the community. You*
> *have six days each week for your ordinary work, but the sev-*
> *enth day must be a Sabbath day of complete rest, a holy day*
> *dedicated to the* Lord. *Anyone who works on the Sabbath*
> *must be put to death." (Exodus 31:14–15)*

> *"You have six days each week for your ordinary work, but the*
> *seventh day must be a Sabbath day of complete rest, a holy*
> *day dedicated to the* Lord. *Anyone who works on that day*
> *must be put to death." (Exodus 35:2)*

In God's community of followers, there in the desert of Sinai, you either kept the Sabbath or you were dead. And I balk at the unyielding, harsh judgment. I want—for myself and the Israelites—some latitude, some permission to decide. There is none. It is as plain as the text states.

After years of playing fast and loose with the fourth commandment, I came to this realization: God's punishment for breaking the Sabbath is as much fact as it is consequence. The truth is, when we don't rest, we die. When we don't reorient back to God, back to the maker of our days, we're walking corpses. We don't bear his image, we don't express freedom for ourselves and others, and we live small, limited lives. Our breath continues, but the source of our life is gone.

I don't want death. I want life. And yet sometimes even my faith life seems to work against me as I seek a Sabbath rest. I consider Scriptures such as "never stop praying" (1 Thessalonians 5:17) or "run with endurance the race God has set before us" (Hebrews 12:1). I think of the virtuous woman of Proverbs 31, and there is a strong temptation to embrace action instead of rest. We must remember—I must remember—that all these statements were made in the context of a time when culture itself provided a rhythm of rest. As Adele Ahlberg Calhoun reminds us in "A Woman of Virtue" about the world of the Proverbs 31 woman: "This woman didn't own a watch or live by a 24/7 pace. When it was dark, everyone went to bed. . . . For all her doing, she lived life within healthy rhythms and limits."

And so can we. So must we, if we are to live. Not only that, but I'm convinced that honoring the Sabbath makes time "bend in your favor"—to borrow a phrase from author Emily P. Freeman. For me, a Sabbath day where activity ceases has led for me, paradoxically (but so like God!) to more time. I believe it is because in honoring God, we come back to the realization that we are eternal. This is not all the time we have. God is not holding out on us. He has offered us all the time we crave, lavishly and abundantly. All we have to do is choose it.

> **As you study this chapter, think about what eternity means to you—what being eternal will mean for you. What does it offer you?**

1. Chances are there are many reasons you can, and have, given yourself for why you can't rest a full twenty-four hours. List all the reasons you have given yourself. Now, for each reason, follow the result of not resting all the way to its logical conclusion. For example, perhaps you are the primary caregiver for a parent. Let's say you continue, every day, to care for others without a break. What is the result for you and for them?

2. For each reason given above, ask yourself if today the choice was to die or stop, could you find a solution?

3. In the book of Nehemiah, the prophet is in the process of two great building projects: the rebuilding of Jerusalem's wall and the rebuilding of God's people. The people have forgotten their identity, and as a result Nehemiah reports in 13:15–18 that he "saw men of Judah treading at their winepresses on the Sabbath." He also saw all the normal acts of commerce taking place, with men bringing goods into the city to sell. What was his solution in verse 19? Think about your own temptations to go about the Sabbath as a normal day. In what ways could you adopt Nehemiah's response?

4. Consider the elasticity of time. Think of times in your life when time stretched out, feeling like a broad expanse to be lived in instead of a tool to be pressed into service. What were you doing? What were you *not* doing?

5. In *Receiving the Day*, Dorothy Bass tells us the Sabbath has "sustained Jewish identity over the centuries, even amid terrible adversity." A saying confirms that "more than the Jews have kept Shabbat, Shabbat has kept the Jews." Consider for yourself how keeping the Sabbath can "keep" you.

6. On your next Sabbath day of rest, turn off the computer, turn off your phone (if possible), don't check e-mails, turn off the television and any other distraction. Read Exodus 33:14 below and think about what the Lord's promise to Moses means for you.

"The LORD replied, 'I will personally go with you . . . and I will give you rest—everything will be fine for you." (Exodus 33:14).

Points to Ponder

In "Sacred Selfishness and Calling" (*Everyday Matters Bible for Women*), Kerri Wyatt Kent tells of a mentor who reminds her, "You have all the time you need to do the things God has called you to do."

- Let that concept sink deep into your mind. Our God is the creator of time, of an evening and morning cycle of twenty-four hours. He, as creator of your day, is not going to require you somehow to produce more time so that more can be done. What can you do to make this a reality in your life?

- If you're in the phase of parenting children, you know the most unrestful hour of the week comes right before church on Sunday. Getting everyone ready to worship, getting there on time, can suck every good intention of a Sabbath rest right out of you. In this case, what other day can serve as your day of rest?

*"Sabbath is, among other things, an invitation
to periodically step out of the relentless stream of
chronos in the hope of catching a whiff of kairos.
It's a willingness to see time as a gift that need not
be managed or maximized but simply enjoyed."*
—Carolyn Arends, "Play!"
Everyday Matters Bible for Women

Prayer

Eternal God, you have created me in your image. You have created me to enjoy your presence forever. Help me see time as a gift from you, to be used for your glory.

Add your prayer in your own words.

Amen.

Put It into Practice

One way we keep time from becoming only what we see and remaining something we know to be eternal is to hold it lightly, to find ways when we lose track of time altogether. And, as Carolyn Arends suggests, one of the best ways to do that is to embrace play—to "consider the spiritual practices of snowboarding, Scrabble, or sandcastle building." What makes you lose track of time? This week, put play back in your Sabbath rest.

Take-away Treasure

One way work remains present in our lives, even as we try to take a Sabbath, is by the physical reminders we have around us. Your briefcase, your backpack, your laundry basket—look around today at all the items that speak of "work" to you. This week on your Sabbath, remove them all from sight. Give your eyes a Sabbath rest as well.

CHAPTER 4

Sabbath Habits

Living a God-Paced Life

"Keep the Sabbath day holy.
   Don't pursue your own interests on that day,
but enjoy the Sabbath
   and speak of it with delight as the LORD's
      holy day.
Honor the Sabbath in everything you do on that day,
   and don't follow your own desires or talk idly.
Then the LORD will be your delight.
   I will give you great honor
and satisfy you with the inheritance I promised
      to your ancestor Jacob.
I, the LORD, have spoken!"

ISAIAH 58:13-14

For this study, read Psalm 23.

When I began to take seriously the fourth commandment, I would have told you the biggest obstacle was my three children and all their needs. From their daily care and maintenance to birthday parties and soccer games, this would be the crux of my Sabbath rest struggle. Yet in the end, it turned out my biggest challenge was myself and my habitual "unrest." I was just so used to working, whether I was at the office or at home. The rut in my life named "work" was so deep and smooth that it was a Herculean effort to lift myself out of it, even for a day. I will admit to a great deal of anxiety as I looked ahead at a good twelve hours with no productivity in sight. Now I can smile at the irony of it, but I remember thinking, quite seriously as I committed to a day of rest each week, "What am I going to *do*?"

In the end, to answer my question, I had to think back to things I remembered enjoying years ago, before play and rest had been crowded out. I made a list, mindful that I was going to be tempted, often, to convince myself there was nothing else to do anyway, and so why not get a bit more work done? The list would be a reminder of things that brought me joy, ways that helped me connect with God's creation. Playing the piano, sitting in the garden (not weeding, just sitting), riding my bicycle—I hadn't done any of these in years!

Yet the discipline of Sabbath rest is a discipline of much more than play, more than doing what we'd like to do. In Isaiah 58, God tells us, "Don't pursue your own interests on that day." In "A Benefit of Obedience" (*Everyday Matters Bible for Women*), Kelli Trujillo writes that "in Scripture we see that true rest is tied inextricably to obedience." It's a discipline that requires us to be attentive, first and foremost to God, to what he is doing and how he is working. We need a God-paced life, and we need habits to help us keep that pace. (And if you have to start with a list, so be it.)

One of the best Sabbath habits is prayer, and for me the unofficial prayer of all Sabbath-keepers is Psalm 23. As Cynthia Heald says in "A God-Paced Life" (*Everyday Matters Bible for Women*), "When the Lord is our shepherd, we have everything we need, so we don't have to worry. . . . Leading a God-paced life means allowing the Lord to be our guide so that we can go on the right paths that honor his name." Psalm 23 helps us focus on God's provision for our lives and calmly, steadily, shows us how secure we are if we follow our shepherd. It is a psalm that reminds us that our only real work is following him.

The spiritual disciplines of meditating on God's word and contemplation can also be used to keep us centered on God. Consider choosing a psalm such as Psalm 91, 95, or 100, considering each word, allowing God's word to lead you into thoughts of his work in your life and gratitude for his world.

For some, a period of silence is what brings about a Sabbath rest; for others it may be songs of praise. Perhaps we need to bring both into our Sabbath days. But more than anything, this is a day where the hardest habit will be the habit of *not* doing. Not planning, not producing, not preparing, not directing the days of others, not worrying about our own days. Not dreaming of relief, but allowing God to restore. It is a day of dwelling in the house of the Lord, your true home. And in that space, as Susan Arico writes in "Addicted to Productivity" (*Everyday Matters Bible for Women*), "We invite God to lead us in how we spend our time, conscientiously choosing to do what God directs, not more, not less."

> *As you study this chapter, think about daily,
> weekly, and seasonal habits you have that help
> you honor God's rhythm of work and rest. Think
> about the habits you've developed that hinder such
> a rhythm. How can you help to shape a pattern
> of living that keeps your attention on God?*

1. For you, what are other spiritual disciplines—such as prayer, contemplation, Bible study, community and so on—that could help you observe the Sabbath? What are the disciplines that reorient your attention to God?

2. Matthew 12:1–13, Mark 2:23–3:6, and Luke 6:1–10 all record how Jesus offended the Pharisees twice—by eating grain as he and the disciples went through a field on the Sabbath and by healing a man's hand. In response to the protests by the Pharisees, he reminds them of the words of Hosea 6:6. When you read the verse in Hosea and consider the actions of Christ on the Sabbath, what motivations should be kept front and center as we create habits to honor the Sabbath?

3. In the Gospel of John we have a passage that can be confusing. We know we are to rest on the Sabbath because God rested, but in John 5:16–17, we read, "So the Jewish leaders began harassing Jesus for breaking the Sabbath rules. But Jesus replied, 'My Father is always working, and so am I.'" Read through the rest of the passage, and consider Jesus' words in the other Gospel accounts that "the Son of Man is Lord, even over the Sabbath." What do we know about God's preeminence as a result?

4. In Psalm 23 we read that our shepherd "guides us along right paths," which bring honor to his name. Cynthia Heald suggests that we can "take our schedules, commitments, and relational demands before God and sincerely ask, *Lord, what is it you want me to focus on? How best can I take time to rest?*" When you read Psalm 23, how do you see the Sabbath as part of God's shepherding care?

5. In Mark 2:27, Jesus reminds us that "the Sabbath was meant to meet the needs of the people, and not people to meet the requirements of the Sabbath." What are the needs you have that can only be met, or met best, by Sabbath rest?

6. Lauren Winner writes in "What Does It Mean to Keep the Sabbath Holy?" (*Everyday Matters Bible for Women*) that on the Sabbath "I try to do things that will give me and God joy." What brings both you and God joy on the Sabbath?

Points to Ponder

As I sought to make the Sabbath a different day, a day of no work for myself or others, I was surprised to realize how much of my conversation with my children revolved around making work for them. My sentences were peppered with phrases such as *pick up, put away, don't forget,* and *come here.* One of the first habits I had to incorporate was a Sabbath rest for my speech.

- What about you? If you weren't telling your family what to do and what was needed, would you be connecting with them?

One of the benefits of a habit is that it doesn't involve thinking—it's just something we do because we've trained ourselves to do it. We understand the benefits of habits when it comes to eating right, exercising, and all sorts of good health guidelines, but we tend to ignore them when it comes to our life with God. Yet getting in the habit of a Sabbath rest is one of the best ways to ensure we take it. We don't always *feel* like resting, but our feelings are not the issue. God's desire to give us rest is our motivation.

- Consider how you created good habits in other areas of your life. How can you use them to work on a healthy Sabbath habit?

"Once you have begun to experience solitude and silence, you discover that you actually have a soul and that there is a God. Then you can begin to practice Sabbath and that will enable you to re-enter community. You can't have community without Sabbath." —Dallas Willard

Prayer

LORD, you are my shepherd; I have all that I need. You let me rest in green meadows; you lead me beside peaceful streams. You renew my strength. You guide me along right paths, bringing honor to your name. "Even when I walk through the darkest valley, I will not be afraid, for you are close beside me. Your rod and your staff protect and comfort me. You prepare a feast for me in the presence of my enemies. You honor me by anointing my head with oil. My cup overflows with blessings. Surely your goodness and unfailing love will pursue me all the days of my life, and I will live in the house of the LORD forever" (Psalm 23).

Add your prayer in your own words.

Amen.

"Most of the things we need to be most fully alive never come in busyness. They grow in rest." —Mark Buchanan, The Holy Wild: Trusting in the Character of God

Put It into Practice

In "Mary Magdalene: Meeting the Risen Lord" (*Everyday Matters Bible for Women*), Jonalyn Fincher suggests two questions to help frame what our Sabbath habits should be. First, ask yourself "What feels like work to me?" and make a list. Then ask yourself, "What would I do if all my work was done?" and make a list. Whether your work is actually done or not, the second is your Sabbath list. As she says, "Most of the time, rest doesn't come handed to us on a platter. We have to choose it." Today, make your lists. And when the Sabbath comes, choose something to do, or be, that doesn't feel like work.

Take-away Treasure

The discipline of Sabbath rest is one of the easiest to talk ourselves out of, partly because our tasks feel easier to do than find a way that leads to rest. Maybe it's your only day to do the shopping. Is it? Or would it mean shifting a week-night routine around so it could be done then? As God says so often, we have six days to do all our work. What is needed is a new way of looking at the week. This week, create a calendar with only six days in the week and make your plans using it.

Notes / Prayer Requests

_____

_____

_____

_____

_____

_____

_____

_____

_____

_____

_____

_____

_____

_____

_____

_____

_____

_____

_____

Notes / Prayer Requests

_____

_____

_____

_____

_____

_____

_____

_____

_____

_____

_____

_____

_____

_____

_____

_____

_____

_____

Leader's Guide

Thoughts on Where to Meet

- If you have the chance, encourage each group member to host a gathering. But make sure your host knows that you don't expect fresh baked scones from scratch or white-glove-test-worthy surroundings. Set the tone for a relaxed and open atmosphere with a warm welcome wherever you can meet. The host can provide the space and the guests can provide the goodies.

- If you can't meet in homes, consider taking at least one of your meetings on the road. Can you meet at a local place where people from your community gather? A park or a coffee shop or other public space perhaps.

- If you meet in a church space, consider partnering with another local church group and take turns hosting. How can you extend your welcome outside your group?

Thoughts on Ways to Foster Welcome

- If many of your members have a hard time meeting due to circumstances, look for ways to work around it. Consider providing childcare if there are moms who have difficulty attending, or meet in an accessible space if someone who might want to join has a disability. Does a morning time work better? Could you meet as smaller groups and then get together as a larger group for an event? Be flexible and see how you can accommodate the needs of the group. Incorporate "get to know you" activities to promote sharing. Don't take yourselves too seriously and let your humor shine through.

Incorporating Other Practices

- *Lift your voices.* Integrate worship throughout the study. Find songs that speak of Sabbath rest.

- *Commit to lift each other up in prayer.* You may want to have a prayer walk as part of seeing opportunities to serve in your community, or prayer partners who might be able to meet at other times.

- *Dig deep into the word.* Take the study at your own pace but consider including passages for participants to read in between meetings. The *Everyday Matters Bible for Women* has a wealth of additional resources.

- *Celebrate!* Bring cupcakes and candles, balloons or anything celebratory to distribute to each member of the group. Ask each person to share something that they want to celebrate today, be it an event, a new insight, or anything they choose.

Sabbath Rest

The discipline of Sabbath rest will pose a unique challenge to you as a leader. It's hard to think of ways to talk about rest and the cessation of our actions! But be encouraged—the study of the Sabbath is richly rewarding and will benefit your group in profound ways. It will also be a study you'll find yourself turning back to again and again as you study other disciplines. Here are a few suggestions as you lead:

- Allow the group to talk about the chaotic schedules they find themselves in, but come to the meeting with a few phrases to help redirect back to how they can change. Ask them: "How does it feel when you're that busy?" or "If you were going to do your schedule over again, what would you change?"

- Keep any detail-oriented questions open-ended, with the possibility of many "right" answers.

- Ask your group to talk about times when they felt their lives contained a true rhythm of rest. Ask them to describe the emotions that come to mind when they think of those times.

- Pray before you meet and then as a group for a discussion free of judgment. We can easily fall into the comparison trap when it comes to how we spend our time and how "godly" our experiences are. We must remember that our Adversary would like nothing

better than to pull us apart, for us to stop meeting together to encourage one another. Your goal is growth
of disciples. Create, with God's help, an atmosphere of
no judgment, but also one that challenges each member to pursue righteousness with her whole heart.

- Use visual tools to provide an added anchor to your
  discussions. Bring in a calendar of six day weeks for
  the group to work with. Bring in items that help you
  to worship—perhaps music or a natural element such
  as a shell.

- Listen to the needs of the group. Your group may be
  discussing Sabbath-keeping at a time when one member is struggling to understand how critical rest is for
  her. Be open to the working of the Spirit to use your
  group to seek God's favor, to grow God's kingdom
  together.

- Add other spiritual disciplines to your discussions. As
  you study, consider also the disciplines of Bible study
  and meditation, solitude, contemplation, celebration,
  prayer, gratitude, and worship.

Follow-Up

Each of us is on a journey of discipleship. We will all at-
tempt things that fail or stumble our way through our
service to God. As your group finishes your time together,
make sure to stay in touch and encourage one another.

Additional Resources

- *24/6* by Matthew Sleeth

- *Hands-Free Mama* by Rachel Macy Stafford

- *Mudhouse Sabbath* by Lauren Winner

- *Receiving the Day: Christian Practices for Opening the Gift of Time* by Dorothy C. Bass

- *Rest: Living in Sabbath Simplicity* by Keri Wyatt Kent

- *Sabbath Keeping: Finding Freedom in the Rhythms of Rest* by Lynne M. Baab

- *The Rest of God* by Mark Buchanan

- She Reads Truth (www.shereadstruth.com)

EVERYDAY MATTERS BIBLE STUDIES
for women

Spiritual practices for everyday life

Acceptance	Mentoring
Bible Study & Meditation	Outreach
Celebration	Prayer
Community	Reconciliation
Confession	Sabbath Rest
Contemplation	Service
Faith	Silence
Fasting	Simplicity
Forgiveness	Solitude
Gratitude	Stewardship
Hospitality	Submission
Justice	Worship

HENDRICKSON PUBLISHERS

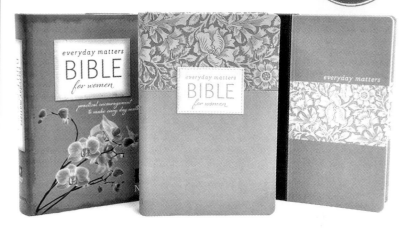